#sharejoy

by: Byron McCoy

BookBaby
7905 North Crescent Boulevard
Pennsauken, NJ 08110
www.BookBaby.com

Print ISBN: 978-1-09830-072-2
eBook ISBN: 978-1-09830-073-9

Printed in the United States of America on SFI Certified paper.

First Edition

TABLE OF CONTENTS

MY REASON

My reason for writing this book is simple. I believe we all have goodness and beauty to share in this world. For some, this shows in the words we speak. For others, it is art, lived acts of love, or an infinitude of other means by which we share ourselves with the world. For me, writing is my means.

In this book, I want to share myself: my joy, love, gratitude, goodwill, and sometimes hurt that color life experience. My experiences are not unique, and in their commonality, I believe they are relatable to others who, in reading, may sense resonance with something in themselves. I want to speak the positivity I see and feel. I want to lift others as others raised me. I want to affirm the good, value, and self-worth we all possess—no matter our circumstance or histories—and most of all, do as the title says: share joy!

That said, this book would not be present if not for my son's request. He finds me writing when he wakes. He knows the journals I carry with me between fields, in farm equipment, and trucks. He asked me to make him a book with my poems. I told him that I would, and from me to him, this is my promise kept.

Sometimes it takes the eyes of a child to return focus to our dreams. My son did this for me. I am indebted to him, my wife, my daughter, and youngest son; as well as to all that inspire, encourage, and give me reason to write and share. I am grateful, too, to God: for the liberties and experiences of my life, for patience, persistence, and the process of faith that led me to discover both a Greater Good and my own personal joy.

To create this book gave me joy, and I am grateful now to share it with you.

#sharejoy

MINDSET
You have the good.
You have the light;
The gift to do
And make things right.

Greatness is within you,
And greatness you will show.
Right now, it is still shaping,
But, one day, the world will know.

SOURCE OF JOY

If we feel a source of joy,
Why would we keep it in?
Might not its sharing be just what
Is needed by a friend?

Why would we want to hide away
Our moments lived most bright;
Then wonder why our world today
Shows so little light?

If we feel a source of joy:
Live it, share, then give away;
Such are little moments made
That give brightness to our days.

BE A LIGHT

Be a light in this world
That others seek to find.
Be a light in this world;
Let your spirit shine.

Find the fire lit within
Which keeps the spirit strong,
That, sometimes, may take time to find
But is present all along.

Find the source that gives you joy,
That shows in what you do.
Share such glow so all may know
The gifts that are of you.

You are a light in this world.
This is clear to me.
You are a light in this world
        and know
It's more than I that sees.

SHARED SPARKS

Seek the souls that spark your own
Kindling friendship into flame
And to the ones that raise you up
Try and do the same.

Together, we are better
Than we ever are as one;
And laughing, sharing, showing joy
With others is more fun

Than saved alone, within the mind,
For too long a length in time;
So seek the ones that break you free
And help your soul to see:

The goodness that we know exists;
The fellowship we know persists;
When friends are found and made and formed
And in shared sparks, souls lit and warmed

Then left to glow for others too
So they might find the same from you.

WHAT WE SEEK

When you travel all the world
Do you find that which you seek,
Or in post-high after-thrill
Feel, still, an absence underneath?

Is it life experience, sentiment, or soul
The spirit needs and active-seeks
To make itself feel whole?

Maybe it is different to every one of us.
I pursued this world's promises.
I chased glory, war, and lusts;
And of each and every one of these
None ever proved enough.

So I went the other way,
Seeking joy within,
And through soul-shadows sensed a light
And purpose to my life:

To give as I am able,
To serve where I am called,
To see that good is everywhere:
…God present after all.

SIMPLE

I try and write it fancy,
Wanting to impress,
But it's only when I'm simple
That I know I said it best.

I am nothing fancy,
But I'm steady and I'm true.
I'll tell you all that's in my mind
If you ever ask me to;

Saying what I see in you,
What I believe that you will be,
Wanting to make good for you,
Thinking less of me.

I will never wow the world
In scintillated extravagance,
But I'll shine in my own way
Living the present-tense.

I am nothing great,
But I know that I am good.
If I can raise another up,
Then I think I should.

YOU INSPIRE ME

You inspire me.
I hope that's plain to see.
Maybe it sounds foolish,
But you raise a better me:

Doing my best to be a light,
To give and share my heart;
Living, writing, joy I feel:
A simple, honest, start.

I hope your day is beautiful,
Whatever you may do.
Thank you for the inspiration
That is the Light in You.

GIVING GRACE

Give the little that we have;
Feel our own voids filled.
Tend to the aid of others;
Witness our own wounds healed.

See the mysteries that become
When our first acts are love:
How we receive in return
That which we give away
To others who—the world may claim—
We do not owe a thing.

But that is love. It is not won,
Has no cost, is given free;
Without condition or demand
Something should be for me.

Its power holds not in force,
Nor influence from outside,
But in the way it changes hearts
When, within them, it resides;

Then propagates in further acts
As soul's seen done to it,
Perpetuating further good
So one does not forget

The way their own world once was changed
By another's selfless act:
That moved a heart and changed one's eyes
And made their soul react.

This is how the world is changed
Humbly, engagement face-to-face.
This is how we raise the world
And spread Love’s giving grace.

WHAT WE FIND

Life's too short not to make
A friend we see right there,
When all that it may take of us
Is simply show we care;

To take a risk and say something
That we wish to share;
That shows to them, in this world,
We are witness to them there

And want to be a friend,
If they'd like to share their time;
Then, right before our very eyes,
A friend is what we find.

MELANCHOLY BURNS AWAY

Is it wrong to love the rain;
The way it turns us cold,
Falls upon a world of gray,
Holding light at bay:

The way it brings back into mind
Hardships of the past,
That, too, turned us cold and cruel
But could neither hold, nor last.

It's just a storm. It's just a front
That will roll through then away:
A swing in life, of tempest's might,
That dims but cannot not blight

Enduring light that, even when blocked,
Behind the clouds still shines;
And will restore the world from gray
When melancholy burns away.

LAY IT ON

If you're having a bad day
Lay it all on me.
That's what I am here for—
To love the sides no others see:

To love in times of trial,
To love when times get tough,
To love when life gets in the way
And nothing seems enough.

I am here, and always will be,
For as long as I might live.
This is the vow I made to you
And honor I will give.

Lay your burden on my back;
Please let me carry too
The weight that holds your spirit down
And was never meant for you.

Let me help you in your life,
Help you through your time,
Until this moment, too, is past
And joy, again, we find.

BEHIND THE FRONT

Do not be ashamed of tears.
They simply show you care;
That you're trying and aware
Of emotions that are there.

Do not worry should they fall.
Somedays, the world needs rain,
And, like a front, behind will be
Clear eyes and skies again;

And if you feel like smiling,
Celebrate that too;
Whether true, or just to fool,
It still is nice on you.

IN THE FALL

There is something special in the fall
When true colors show;
To see another in a light
You've always wished to know.

Fleeting, brief, as it may be,
We are blessed to see
True colors always present
Yet hidden underneath
Attempts to be like all the rest—
    lost in a sea of green.

In this season and your change,
I witness how you glow,
Enchanted with your beauty
That evermore does show.

I see the way that you stand out,
The way your spirit shines,
And wonder how I did not see
Your presence all this time.

A TRUE FRIEND

My youngest son talks on and on
About his greatest friend:
Of all he's done—and plans to do—
Whenever he's with him;

Adventures, swimming, funny faces;
At home, in parks, or to new places.
Even, to me, it brings much joy
To see such brightness in a boy;

Reminding me what friends can give
To any life, wherever lived,
When shared with ones that lift us up;
That, to have such, is well enough

To raise us all when we may stumble,
Make us bold when we are humble,
Laugh and smile when before were sad:
That he has this, I am glad.

I love to see his little mind
Value what's deserved;
To see him grow out from his shell,
No longer meek, reserved.

Now running wild, they both go
In fun and friendship they full show
And share and spread around
To us who see, and find again,
What joy abounds in a true friend.

THE GOODNESS THAT I SEE

I hope to be your friend.
How to show? I wouldn't know.
For years I never tried, content
With the few I hold.

But people change and people grow,
As does the world around,
And in the living of our days
Kind souls are seen and found:

Some that pass right through our lives,
Like foil characters in plays,
While others hold and find a place
And in our lives remain.

I hope to be your friend
For the goodness that I see
And the simple kindness that you show
To all—including me.

JUST HAPPY

I'm not seeking answers
To questions I won't ask.
I'm just happy with my life;
Where I feel that it's at.

I don't need to know the ending,
Nor the way that it will write;
What's meant to be will be,
And that will come in time.

SOMETHING TOO

Why is it so hard sometimes
Simply to be real:
To share and show to others
What it is we truly feel;

To offer them our honest thoughts,
Meant only to be kind,
And say that in our busy day
They were on our mind?

Why is this so hard some days
For us to simply do
When the thought, to them as well,
Could mean something too?

Byron McCoy

WAR STORY

I went to war expecting death
And when it didn't come
It happened, then, in aftermath—
When I came undone.

I expected Hell, found something else,
Returned a better man,
Then found it was in idleness
The Devil played his hand:

Drink and chase and keeping pace
With what we're told to seek
Upset my soul and dulled my mind
To even stop and think

Why I did the things I did,
The reason I exist,
Then through my darkness
    shone a light:
"There's more to life than this."

So I changed, returned to serve
But in a different way.
This became again my light
For living every day.

To die in sacrificial Love, the greatest honor
In war's wicked game:
How much more could we achieve
If we lived, too, for the same?

#sharejoy

Service, Love, and quiet truths
Untold (for so many want only
Tales of war and glory),
It's for our Brothers, all we Love,
That is the Greater Story.

It does not matter what becomes.
It matters how we live:
Our dignity, compassion, Love
That we daily give.

There's more to me. There's more to you
Than ever meets the eye,
But maybe we will see more true
In letting our light through

To illuminate life's simple truth
We know and then forget;
To see again what once was clear:
That Good is present, everywhere.

ALL THAT MATTERS

If that's all that matters
Then I'm on a better track
Than I was, in years before,
If honest, looking back.

I loved the service that I gave
But saw no purpose in campaign;
Witnessing sacrifice, for what?
There was nothing there to gain.

I lived for others, lost myself;
At times for me and no one else.
Both extremes left me down.
Today,
I'm nearer to a balance found.

I love the times I labor
Alone in open space
Where I am left all to myself,
To mind, and God's world grace.

I love to see my labor
Raise bounty from the soil:
Man's work since His beginning
Garden
And source for all since toil.

I love my thoughts. I love to share,
Especially with ones that care;
Who wish to know parts of me
That, absent words, are hard to see.

#sharejoy

I am happy with what I do.
I'm happy how I live.
I'm happy that I've found a way
Of myself to give

Goodwill and sentiments that
In past I would withhold;
Stories, thoughts, experience
That would have stayed untold

But now believe are worth the time
To write and show and share
Because, maybe, they might help another
And, for that, I want them there.

We are not alone in this world,
No matter how we feel,
And when we're left in solitude
Sometimes it's hard to heal

When what we need is affirmation,
Someone to say we'll be alright
—Because they've been right where we are—
Is reason that I write.

Sometimes it's hard for me to speak
All the love I feel;
But when I stop and write it down,
That also makes it real

And present in the world
For whoever may then need
To know that they are not alone
Through words, from me, they read.

*"If you're happy with what you do…
It's all that matters!"* True!
One of my life's greatest joys
Is to write and share with you.

If that's all that matters,
Then I'm better than I've been.
I want to say what needs told
And be a better friend

To whoever may be searching
For someone that wants to share;
Same as I searched in years before:
For you, these words are there.

THE DRIVE

I do not know my destination,
    where it is I'll end,
Nor even if this road I'm on
Is where I should begin;

If I've been steady now for years
Along my fated path,
Or if, time soon, a change will come
And sudden alter track.

I'll read the signs as best I can
(That doesn't make me right)
And should I learn my way is wrong,
I'll change with altered sight.

How will we know? I couldn't say
This is my only drive,
But—to travel on this road—
I'm glad to be alive.

GOOD TIMES

No it ain't always sunny days.
Sometimes life turns cold and gray
And troubles, they, won't stay away.
Just tough it out and see it through;
Good times are coming back to you.

Winters come and winters go.
Cold winds will blow and sometimes snow.
Fair weather birds, they fly away;
Those that are true, they'll hold and stay.
Just tough it out and see it through;
Good times are coming back to you.

Trust me son, I've been there too;
Good times are coming back to you.
May not see it now, but man I do!
Good times are coming back to you.

THE THINGS WE NEVER SAY

Funny all that we can write
From words we hide away;
The things we long for most to share
But never seem to say;

That, when we hear, seem too raw;
From us, feel too deep;
So we tuck them back away
And, with our secrets, keep.

Then we write them different.
Allusion masks the real:
Softening the way they hit,
Weakening their feel.

Yet what we sense remains unchanged,
Even when not shown.
Then, alone, we wonder why
Our truth is never known.

Funny all that we can write
As, another, I begin,
And when it does not come out right
I know I'll try again.

HOPEFUL FRIEND

I think that you are beautiful.
I see that you are kind.
Maybe these are reasons why
You are on my mind.

Your eyes, they hold a special gleam,
A happiness that's real,
And when you are upon a scene
There is a presence others feel:

That leads sad eyes to shine,
New smiles to spread and break,
From a kind and warming sense
Your spirit seems to make.

I say such things as hopeful friend,
With kind affinity,
To say these words I write and share
Are foremost felt in me.

UNSEEN
I feel that we are similar
In ways hard to define—
In how we think, our hearts respond,
The way we live our lives:

The way we love for others
And, quiet, show our care;
Never intending to stand out;
Willing to go without

If, by so, the ones we love
Discover their own joy.
For this is how we give ourselves
To friends, to girls, and boys;

Sharing time and subtle signs
That grow into something more;
Realized, only with time,
In what we leave behind:

The memories and stories
Others tell of us.
But today, we're humble still
And, in future day, hold trust

That it will say and show
What today appears so small:
That love is what we always gave,
Unseen, but present all along.

LIFE'S WORTH (FATHER TO A SON)

I don't need to make a million.
I don't need to make a dime.
Today we bought a memory
Whose cost was only time:

Catch in the backyard, home runs into fields
Memories of childhood with simple, honest thrills.
"Nice toss…good hit!" and compliments
That build up, and don't tear down,
A fundamental confidence
Where life success is found.

I don't need to make a million.
I don't need to make a dime.
What I wish to buy are memories—
In the moments that we gave—
And money cannot buy such things
If time is never made.

So work can wait another day.
Have you been outside?
These are the kind of afternoons
    that (to me) define
What it is to feel alive.

I don't need to make a million,
Not even one or two;
The gifts I wish to give of me
Are moments lived with you.

2 A.M.

Another night, I strain to sleep,
And so I clear my mind;
Writing down the thoughts it keeps
Line by leading line.

Lord, thank you for this life:
My children and my wife;
Know even when I get it wrong
I'm trying to do right.

I pray for all those in the world
Who may, too, be like me:
Restless spirits seeking still
the full
Of who they're meant to be.

My eyes are open. I will work
And follow when I see;
Lord help me be a better man
As you call me to be.

AFFECT JUST ONE

Maybe I am simple,
Will never become much,
But to know just who I am,
Itself, is still enough.

I will live my life aligned
To Goodness as I see.
If it has little effect
That still is fine by me:

For if I live it honest,
If I live it true,
Perhaps I may affect just one,
And maybe it is you.

DAYLIGHT DIE

Have you witnessed daylight die
And felt the same in you:
When fading glory, wonder, light
Leaves you only blue?

I've felt this way, once or twice,
Before Dark Nights of the Soul;
Mourning over all the light
It seemed the world had stole.

Then, it went the other way,
From darkness drew a glow,
Hinting at a coming dawn
And warmth my heart would know.

This is a cycle of our world,
A reminder every day,
That no matter what we feel in loss
All will be okay.

The sun will rise. The sky will glow.
Light, again, will break and show
And out of darkness, we will see
All is as it's meant to be.

SOLSTICE

With little note, the sky is changed.
Light extends its time;
And the longest darkness of our nights
Now are days behind.

The change, it happens subtle,
But that is all it takes
To begin the cycle
Where our world, again, will wake:

When life rises from the Earth,
Spreads amongst the trees,
And the darkness of our winter
Becomes but memory.

FROM AFAR
I know I only see you
In busy rooms and from afar,
Yet every time I do
I wonder how you are.

Studying your presence,
The way that you stand out,
I wonder private, to myself,
What you are all about.

Maybe I will learn one day,
Become a closer friend.
Until then I'll wonder
And keep my thoughts within.

I'll wonder if, perhaps, you too
Feel a draw to me:
An awareness unexplained,
Sensed but never seen.

Maybe I will learn one day:
Discover who you are.
Until then I will remain
Admiring from afar.

BETTER

Some things go better together…
Like sun-tanned legs and summer nights,
Wine-kissed lips and moonshined eyes;
Takes me back to another time
When I was hers and she was mine.

Some things go better together…
Like broken hearts and seeing things
For what they really are;
'Cause you can't have more
When you're holding on
To everything that you knew before.

Some things go better together…
Like lonely roads and times that grow,
Clearing mind and leaving past behind;
Never know what we might find.

Some things go better together…
Like a smile and that light in your eyes,
Having a friend that just feel right;
Makes you want to say all you held inside.

Some things go better together…
And some just make you better.

LITTLE LIGHT

You said to be a light
And, in that, I felt your shine;
Being witness to your own
Gave rekindling to mine.

Even if it never shows
And the world it never sees,
Your smile and your kindness, then,
Had effect on me.

It's funny how one simple act
May aid another on their way.
"Thank you for the little light,"
Is all I wished to say.

BETTER MAN

I used to be ashamed
Of the ways that I would feel,
Pretend I didn't know
Emotions that were real.

I mistook affinity of soul
For attraction to the flesh
And in misguided understanding
Felt shame and mental mess

Until it cleared and I saw true
What it was I loved of you
And you, and you, and you as well—
Attraction to a life lived well:

Of joy shown and seen on face,
Of kindness shared and friendship's grace.
I did not understand back then
That what I sought was a soul-friend

Which can be sensed before its learned,
Given free, and needs not earned.
I see it now and understand.
For this, I am a better man.

GIVE MY THOUGHTS

If I overshare, that would be a change
From all the years I never spoke
Or gave hint to anything.

Maybe I am older.
Maybe I'm more wise
From lessons learned
    and living life
To better realize

That if I want to make a friend
I must extend a hand.
Whether it is taken up
Is not for my command.

How can one know what we won't say,
What we refuse to share?
What insanity is that, to expect
Another knows it there?

I've learned my voice, know who I am,
And to both be true.
This is why I write right now
And give my thoughts to you.

SHARE THE MOMENTS

It’s amazing how a few kind words
Can turn a day around;
How in a day of darkness
A point of light be found.

Through thoughts and sentiments,
Seldom shared before,
A spirit is raised higher
In hope for something more:

To have found a friend,
With shared interests and like-soul,
And by such discovery,
In this world, feel less alone.

Share the moments when we’re touched.
It’s not for us to know,
How our affections—drawn to share—
May greater raise with whom they’re shown.

I WILL PRAY

That's not what I expected
Beginning my day in the dark.
I smiled to your family's faces
Believing it a joyous start;
Then reading on, I learned the greater
Gravity of heart.

I'll pray for you from this day on
Until a fate is known,
Holding faith in God above
Until His will is shown.

"God writes a beautiful life story,"
it's true;
But, Yours, it is not through!

There holds a greater plan
To be revealed to us one day.
I won't pretend to know it now,
But for it, and You, I pray.

We cannot change what is;
Control only how we live.
I am ever grateful for your light:
The faith example that you give.

I will pray. I will pray,
And I will pray again;
Hoping it may have effect
For one I call a friend.

IT DOESN'T MATTER

Perhaps I, too, am on your mind
Or maybe it's just me.
It doesn't matter either way;
The thought is nice to me.

ALRIGHT

I have my highs.
I have my lows,
My darkness and my light.
Whatever that I am today
I know I'll be alright.

PLAIN DAYS

Not every day is filled with light.
Some days we just get by;
And when we do not feel inspired
That doesn't mean we shouldn't try

To still do good, however plain;
Speak in acts, not words we say;
Remain engaged in world around;
For in plain days, good still is found.

IF WE ONLY KNEW

I've been an angel, been a demon:
I am the human in between.
I've lived the high of knowing Hell
Was something I could bring.

I've hailed the Heavens,
Rained their wrath,
Been one that saved,
And, too, a hand for death.

I've prayed that I was right;
More than a piece in a machine;
That we would further nearer peace
We proclaimed to bring.

I learned life isn't cut and dry,
Not always black and white;
And that it's in the shades of gray
That keep you up at night.

I learned my greatest difference
Was in loving those I served;
Giving to each the Honor
All in this world deserve.

That's what I still try and do:
Respect I show to you.
This life is such a wonder:
If we only knew.

CYCLE ROUND

Highs and lows, they cycle round.
Remember that when you are down;
That darkness comes before the light,
Whatever is, you'll be alright.

No matter what you feel today,
It will change again.
And when it does, whichever way,
There will be another day:

To pick you up, or knock you down;
Remember all comes back around.

CIGAR THOUGHT

When you feel the light about to die,
Take another breath.
We only have so many draws,
Know not the number left.

When you feel the light about to die,
Breathe into it new flame;
Then feel the burn, the way it hits
To warm the soul again.

Feel the burn, the subtle high,
As the sense takes hold.
Don't let it fade away.
Don't let the world leave cold.

Take the moment and reflect
On whatever fills your mind
And, with gratitude, find a peace
In such quiet times.

This is the way I am alone
When I feel burned out.
Still, I breathe another time.
I feel the return high
Knowing such is how it's meant:
The gift to be alive.

SHINE

I know I hardly know you.
But still I sense a light;
One that, I believe, in time
Will only grow more bright;

And when it does, I hope that I
Am near enough to view
The way you shine, the way you glow,
When it shows in you.

Forgive me if I over-speak.
I want only to share
Affinity, as I see,
With ones that affect me.

I hope your day is beautiful.
I hope your day is bright
And, should you feel a little joy,
That you share its light.

AFFIRMATION

Thank you for the little things
You do not know you do;
All the good that comes about
By simply being you.

Know that you are noticed,
That your presence has a hold;
And that you make a difference
Even when you are not told.

GRATITUDE

Gratitude is simple
If we only let it show.
What little does it cost of us
To let another know?

TIME TO GROW

In the rain, take time to grow.
When it's right, beauty will show;
And on that day, all will see
The wonder you are meant to be.

MEEKNESS

Why is it so hard sometimes
To simply say hello;
To go up to another soul
You want so bad to know?

Instead of sharing all it is
That you'd like to say,
You hold it back, save it away,
For another day;

Saying "next time will be different,"
"Next time I will change,"
But how is this to happen
If we do not act today?

Affinity is not for self.
It's meant to share with someone else;
So when you feel it, show it true;
It's meant for them and not for you.

UNSAID
"To see you gave me joy,
Even if it didn't show,
And, right now, I kick myself:
That I did not say hello."

"

I tried to think of words to say:
Finding none, I shied away."

"It's always nice to see you,
Wherever that may be.
There are many lights in this world
And you are one to me."

HELP YOU SHINE

I don't want to steal your light.
I want to help you shine,
Raise you up so that you see
What's been there all this time.

I've lived my days of darkness,
Seasons without sun,
And know that feeling all alone,
Or lost, is never fun.

From those days, I made it through
And know that you will too;
So always know your worth and good
No matter what you do.

Warmer days are coming,
Green and growth again;
And when they do, I hope that you
Will see me as a friend.

A GIFT

Embrace life's inspirations
Wherever they may lie.
Don't pause and wonder too long why
For they will pass us by.

Live the moment; love the life.
Proclaim the joy; endure the strife.
Be grateful for all THIS that IS.
It is a gift—this life we live.

A LIFE OF JOY

When we live a life of joy
It's funny what we find:
That when we see another soul,
Most often it is kind,

That goodness is our standard state
Not evil—a lie we're told
Daily by news cycles
Straining too hard to stay bold

Until we become indifferent
As the shock wears old;
Which shapes world aberrations
Into perceptions of new norms.

I wonder how such messaging
Propagates us further harm
When all that we would have to do
Is affirm a living truth—
That when good is done for others
It is also done in you.

Not with immediacy, perhaps,
As we've been conditioned strong to doubt;
But through repetitioned acts, we see
Goodwill is what we are about.

Then slowly, by the way we live,
We reshape our world around
To the good and light we witness now
And everywhere abounds.

#sharejoy

It's amazing all the good we see
When such is what we seek
And how life's darkness falls away
Where goodness holds and keeps.

When we live a life of joy
It's funny what we find:
That good resides in all of us,
As we discover in due time;

Most often by acts others make
Toward us, and in us wake,
A sense of love in self
That, when lived out, moves furthermore
The heart of someone else.

CAMPFIRE THOUGHTS

Find what makes you happy;
Of the soul and not a high;
Live it up, enjoy it now,
Before the time is by.

Nothing is for certain,
Nothing promised or for sure;
So live the moments that you get
And to others give

What we are able;
Give as we can see;
Share the joy that we sense
And with others live it free.

TURNING IN

Have you ever lit a fire
Just to feel a flame;
To be near its light, watch it burn,
And know such warmth again?

Or do you leave such things alone,
Play it safe and cold,
Never fueling passion light
That burned in youth, now old?

I rest beside the dancing flames.
I love the heat and light.
Then, knowing better,
Turn on in—calling it a night.

A RUN

I took a run to clear my mind,
Disappeared, and hit my stride
Under dark, rain, and pines
Not knowing what, in them, I'd find.

I found I had not lost a step
If I just let go,
Let my body set its pace
Then RUN, not take it slow.

Through the tightness of early miles
My body settled in;
And, like myself in years before,
I was a ghost again.

Alone in woods, an invisible man
Who through the dark could see
Where it was I started out
And where I set to be.

I owned the night, world absent light.
In rain and darkness, I felt right;
A hunter of the night that sought
To fix and shape an unmade thought.

I ran and let it go:
Worries, care, and fear;
And when I stopped to take it in
I found myself right here.

#sharejoy

Alone: but full at peace.

Sometimes when the body aches
In mind, or soul, or heart;
You just have to run
Until it frees or tears apart.

You learn again what you can do
In what you push on through.
These are the times when I run best:
When life throws down its tests.

ADMISSION

Often I pray for almost-strangers,
Those I barely know:
Praying that they learn their good
And let that, of them, show.

For I was once a stranger too,
To myself as well.
I know someone must have prayed for me,
Helped raise me when I fell,

And brought me to a better way
That I still live today.
To all that must've prayed for me,
I'm grateful to this day.

IT CAME TRUE

I prayed for you, and it came true.
For that, know I am glad for you.

YOU ARE SEEN

You matter and are seen
Even when the world won't show;
Good and beauty are within you
And that's all you need to know.

THE PRODIGAL

Welcome back my long, lost friend.
I know it's been a while
Since you've felt the burden freed
And liberty to smile.

Welcome back my long, lost friend.
Another day is here
Where past is past, and future—fate—
Begins anew today.

The day is good, and so are you.
Are you awakened, eyes anew?

Lay down the burden that you've borne,
The pain you only knew.
Know that a future still exists
With joy, designed for you.

Welcome back my long, lost friend.
You've been away too long;
And know that in our circle, small,
You always will belong.

ANOTHER IS AROUND

Sometimes, just to know
Another is around
Is enough to feel a smile
And simple joy be found

That didn't seem to be before
But suddenly is there,
And becomes most what we see
Nearly everywhere.

To know that we are noticed,
Know that we are seen,
Is enough to spark our souls
And kindle lit eyes' gleam.

Embrace affections of the soul
Wherever they may lead.
Perhaps our own shared happiness
Might be another's seed.

SMILE

Funny how a smile
Can brighten a whole day,
Erase a darkness felt before
And keep it far away.

Funny how a smile
Can shine into a soul
And make a sense of emptiness
Feel suddenly more whole.

Why not share a smile
When joy is what we sense?
Does any better way exist
    to spread goodwill
Than the simple act of this?

DEAR TOMORROW

Dear Tomorrow, I know I'll see you.
Sometimes I wish I didn't have to wait.
You know I've been hoping for a little sun
'Cause outside my window, all I see is rain.
This weather we've been having,
You know it's bound to change!

Dear Tomorrow, I'll do my best to do
Those little things that you asked me to;
I'm doing all I can to make it good for you.

Dear Tomorrow, knowing that you're out there,
Raises me up is what I want to say.
Dear Tomorrow, see you when I see you.

Sincerely,
Today

BLOOM

Don't be ashamed, should sad days show;
Remember, it takes rain for crops to grow.
In our days of gray and somber gloom
                    consider
Perhaps they, too, prepare us for bloom.

NOTHING LOST

Nothing's lost and nothing's gained.
The pieces are but rearranged.
So pick them up from where they lay;
It's bound to happen when you play.

So raise your head and keep it high.
There comes another day.
You're never out. It's never done
Until you walk away.

A DIFFERENT RUN

It was a day of rain and gray.
I went running anyway.
Sometimes you just need to move
To lose the ache in you:
To raise up what is buried deep
And bring it forth to see.

The miles raised emotions
Harbored far away.
"You deserve to be happy,"
Is all they seemed to say.

I let them go, cried alone;
Then headed home, no one to know.

A LITTLE FARTHER

Here's to new beginnings,
To miles left behind,
The good that lies ahead,
If willing to seek and find.

So push a little harder.
Give a little more.
Go a little farther.
The dream is still in store.

THINK OF SPRING

Why, in autumn times as these,
Do I think of spring;
Back to sights and senses that
Its season brings to me;

Of walks alone, beneath the trees
And budding canopy
With hidden sights of laurel blooms
Breaking underneath;

That color under-mountainsides
In pastels and pure white;
Absorbing every drop of sun
In filtered mountain light;

Before the summer burns away
And the colors fade;
Then only green is what we see
Until autumn falls away;

When the world again is cast
In shades of different hues:
Of deeper reds and dying golds
Against a backdrop blue.

The colors then, of season's end,
Bring with them different moods;
Maybe this is why I think of spring:
To when the world was new.

ROLLING HARROW

If you've never plugged a rolling harrow
I'd advise you, "Don't begin."
It's hard to dig out anywhere
When mud fuses with stem.

You'll cuss and curse, use words you thought
Were secrets when still small
Then growing up, discover quick
Were not secrets after all!

It'll happen by a road where anyone can view
Giving smile, and a laugh, to everyone but you.
You'll dig and dig. Gloves will fray
And thinking of that mudhole say,
"I should have stayed away!"

Then, when clean, hurriedly
You'll race to start back in.
Then, looking back, near heart attack,
"Oh ..., happened again!"

Now it is dark and still I dig
Working by tractor light.
If I could give some small advice,
"Wait 'til the ground is right."

This poem was written for my children. Its inspiration was reading Shel Silverstein poems before bed.

The day I wrote it, we were working heavy (wet) ground in preparation for winter wheat. The ground was not right, and I spent a good amount of darkness cleaning out the rolling harrow of our tillage implement with a hammer and pry bar.

#sharejoy

It was a frustrating day, but coming home, my children greeted me with love and excitement to read their favorite poems.

It was in one of these bedtime readings when my oldest son asked me to make him a book with my poems. I told him that I would, and this is that book.

Absent his request, this book would not exist. I could not create a book without this poem, inspired by he and his sister reading to me (with their little brother listening in) because—for me—this book is first and foremost a kept promise to my son.

A LITTLE FAITH

Have a little faith.
It will all make sense in time.
Do not let what's still unknown
Trouble well-meant mind.

If it's honest, if it's true,
Why should it worry you?
Live the person that you are.
Do as you're meant to do.

How can we live a life of love
If we never give?
How can we bring good into light
That's left forever hid?

Sometimes it takes being a fool
To begin a better way;
When sanity and better sense
Beseech for us to stay

Fast to what is known,
Fast to what is safe;
When something greater, just beyond,
Is meant to be our place.

If it's for me to be the fool,
I'll let my worries fall.
I will continue on this path;
I'll act as I am called.

#sharejoy

I have a little faith,
And daily it does grow.
While I do not understand today,
I believe, one day I'll know:

Why it is I feel this way;
Why it is I'm drawn;
Why it is I'm called to share;
Why it is I care.

Byron McCoy

AUGER WAGON WONDERINGS

Different fields but the same sky;
What do you do to pass the time?
Do you leave your mind to roam?
If you do, where does it go?

Do you think of what's around,
On something lost, or something found;
Of the future, past, or friend;
Where is it your thoughts begin?

I reflect on all above.
I pray to God; I think on love;
A hopeless dreamer in a field
Grounded in work that keeps me real.

GLOW INTO DAY

I witnessed night glow into day
And thought of you not far away.
Did we share the same sky view?
How did it look and seem to you?

Then, at once, I could see
And, to know, raised light in me.

AFFINITY

Affinity is funny
We choose not for whom its fixed
But when a draw is felt and sensed
We know, precise, to whom it sticks.

Affinity is like a light
That leads to closer view
Another soul to which you're drawn
From sense they spark in you.

Then from affinity's soft flame
We form something with name—
A Friend—one of the greatest gifts
In life that we may gain.

GRATITUDE AND GRATEFULNESS

Gratitude and gratefulness,
Whomever it is for,
Bestows to me a sense of joy:
And desire to share more;

To show and give the good I see,
That which I know to be,
To bring this out, and give to others
All that is in me.

Maybe there's a limit
To the love that we can give;
But even if there is,
I still have much to live.

Thank you to all in this world
Who affirm to me each day
That we all can have effect
In small and simple ways.

THE MAN YOU SEE

I don't believe in make-believe
        at least
Not when it comes to me.
I do my best to live so that
I am the man you see.

FAKE IT 'TIL YOU MAKE IT

"Fake it 'til you make it."
I don't believe in that.
"If someone strikes you,
Strike them back!"
    nor do I follow that.

How can we change a heart
When we do not know our own?
How do we guide another up
If we take not the higher road?

"To thine own self be true,"
As well to all we meet!
For an honest life, lived in light,
Itself is still a feat.

POLISHED

Music was the medium
That made him feel again;
Took him back to lives ago,
Reliving deep and slow;

Turning over memories
Like river-rounded stones;
Learning, knowing every feel
Before he let them go.

The world, it wears us all;
Breaks, or polishes to shine.
Sometimes it feels the one
But in the end, done to us,
The other's what we find.

CHANGE THE WORLD

I wished to change the world
And in doing changed my heart:
Learning that to do such
Was the requisite first start.

WHAT MAKES YOU HAPPY

Live what makes you happy:
It's what I try and do.
One of the things that gives me joy
Is sharing thoughts with you.

Byron McCoy

KEEP ON MOVING

Life is like a run.
It starts out slow…and then we go.
In time, we find our stride.
We settle into pace,
Move past the point where everything
Seems to be a race.

We run to just be better,
Live our life the same;
Know it's more than metrics;
More than a win-loss game.

It ties it all together: body, spirit, mind.
We keep on moving 'til we reach
Where we went to find.
We're better for the miles, better for the run,
And—looking back on covered ground—
Hope we made it fun.

“LIKE”

I never thought a heart-shaped mark
Would mean something to me,
But it always has effect:
To know Someone has seen.

There are times when I write
In hope my words are found;
Then when they are, and I can see,
A joy in me abounds.

To know Someone has read and,
Perhaps, sensed something too,
Means a little more to me
Than others prob’ly knew.

Thank you for your time,
For bringing me into your mind,
I wish that I had more to say
But have run out of rhyme.

IN LIGHT

I'm not one to seek out company.
I'm slow to make new friends,
But for the times I've known you
I hope a friendship will begin.

Your kindness is apparent,
Your thoughtfulness as well,
With goodness all around you
As clear as I can tell.

So if I smile in excess
The reason, I attest,
Is that your presence shines with light
And raises, too, my best.

IN GRATITUDE

Thank you for the little ways
You make another's day:
Kind words, a smile, thoughtfulness,
For letting children play.

I see the light of joy within
My children when near you,
When given time with friends
            your kids
In moments made by you.

Thank you for their smiles,
Their laughs and joyous light,
That by a simple thoughtful act
Your offer made ignite.

I hope that we may soon return
The light of joy and fun
That outward from our own kids shines
By kindness you've begun.

Thank you for your thoughtfulness,
The ways you make another's day:
From children's joy, you made mine too.
In gratitude, thank you
For these little things you do.

BIRTHDAY PRAYER

Another trip around the sun,
I'm grateful for this ride;
That on this winter day I may
Be witness to its rise.

Lord, thank you for all that I have,
The gifts you've given me;
Family, friends, all I know
That help me grow and see.

Lord, may this be another year
Where I may do your good:
Living, giving, sharing love
As I know I should.

Lord, thank you for this life,
This blessing that I live;
Help me to spread your will
In all that I may give.

END OF YEAR REFLECTION

This year, it brought me gain,
Joy and growth and hurt;
And even of the times in pain,
I now see their worth.

The challenges, they build us.
The hurt, it makes us strong;
Moving us towards something greater
Waiting all along.

All that we are meant to have
Will be revealed when right;
Until then, we carry on
Living out life's fight;

Not with malice, not in pain,
Understanding that's the game;
That if we want to know life's spoils
We must embrace, and take, its toils

That often start within ourselves.
Then once we've mastered that,
There is little that remains
To stop and hold us back.

I'm stronger than I was;
More grateful too as well;
Of all that still remains to be:
Only time will tell.

I will embrace the toil.
I will love the fight;
Live and give in gratitude;
Do best to be my light.

NEW YEAR'S WISH

I hope this year is filled with joy,
Light, and better days;
And, for you, I believe
It can be no other way.

Smile when you feel it.
Let the sad roll through.
It is a brand new year
            and
Good days are meant for you.

HONEST, STEADY FEW
I don’t need a crowd or lots of noise
To feel that I belong,
Only a soul that speaks to mine
And says I’m not alone:

That whatever it is I may feel,
Someone has felt it too;
Whatever hardship that I sense,
Another’s seen it through.

I don’t need a million friends,
Just an honest, steady few.
This is how it is for me.
How is it for you?

MAKE A FRIEND

May I see your smile
If only from afar;
To feel the light of warmth and kindness
Illumed by where you are?

May I share a word,
A laugh and simple tale,
That fosters fellowship of friends
And makes a spirit well?

May I enjoy your company
That seems so kind to me
And better know the person that
You appear to be?

Perhaps true, or different too,
I want to learn of you
And share, as well, just who I am.
I want to make a friend.

PASSING THROUGH

What little that I know you
I'm glad you're in my life.
For even in such fleeting time
You still have given light:

Shining brightness in my world,
Guiding me to different views
Never thought, unconsidered,
Until raised by you.

We never know the place we take
In another's mind,
The way we may affect another
In a moment's time

Lived sincerely, lived outright,
In truth that others see,
So it was, and still remains—
The way that you touched me.

POETRY

Poetry—a way to say
The plain another way,
Or intimate at sentiments
Close-held or kept at bay.

Whatever that you feel,
Find way to write it down,
Then share it to the world,
        or Someone,
In whom it may resound

As parallel to how they feel,
Think, dream, or believe,
And by our words, put into form,
In shape Another sees:

A reflection of their own soul's self
Perceived, but found, in no one else,
And suddenly they're less alone
For a like-soul is better known.

When you feel a need to write,
Write it true to self,
And if compelled further to share—
                Do.
Perhaps it, too, will mean
Something to Someone else.

WRITING

If writing brings us nearer
To another's heart and mind,
Isn't that a purpose
Writing seeks to find?

Might it not awaken, too,
Another's sleeping dreams?
I believe it can
Because it did in me.

Byron McCoy

THE ONE THAT GOT AWAY

Excuse me girl, hope you don't mind
But I see you looking round and round the room,
Keep wondering who it is that you're trying to find.
Is he the reason you came out,
Why after every time you search around
Your pretty face and eyes, they fall down?

Yeah he broke your heart? That's a God-damned shame.
He sounds better off as one that got away.
No I don't know him, and I don't know you.
I'd be lying if I said I didn't want to know one of the two.

No I ain't playing games. I ain't making moves;
Just saying that where you are right now,
I've been there too.
Know it ain't today, but one day you'll say
Thank God
For the one that got away.

I know he ain't perfect. No one is.
So don't blame yourself for words unsaid
And all the little things that he kept hid.
No, I ain't preaching. I've lived both sides,
And know it only takes once to get it right!

Know it's not today, but someday you'll see
The greatest thing he ever did for you
Was the day he left and set you free.

#sharejoy

Yeah he broke your heart? That's a God-damned shame.
He sounds better off as one that got away.
No I don't know him, and I don't know you.
I'd be lying if I said I didn't want to know one of the two.

No I ain't playing games. I ain't making moves
But looking out around this room;
Ain't another soul here holds a candle to you.
Know it ain't today, but one day you'll say
        Thank God
For the one that got away.

Don't hide your eyes; I see your shine.
I know that you're still hurting tonight
But in time, everything'll be alright.
Maybe we'll meet again. I hope we do.
Ain't another soul here holds a candle to you.

Those eyes'll dry. A smile will show;
Looking back on this one day, in your heart you'll know
It was one of the best days of your life:
The day he said goodbye.

You've got so much good right up ahead,
I just couldn't see you down and leave that unsaid.

Know it ain't today, but one day you'll say
        Thank God
For the one that got away...

KNOW YOU

Pardon me, please excuse,
I don't mean to be rude;
But I've been across the room,
Can't take my eyes off from you.

What's your name? Where you from?
Won't you tell me what you do?
'Cause
I want to know you; I want to know you;
I want to know you.

I'm not one to be this way.
I don't usually say a thing;
Just a face in a crowd, would never know I was around;
But I saw and I felt and I just couldn't help
Coming up to you, taking my heart from its shelf;
Couldn't let this moment by without even saying Hi
'Cause
I want to know you; I want to know you;
I want to know you.

Don't know how to say a line
So I'll tell it to you true;
Never learned to play it cool,
But
I want to know you; I want to know you;
I want to know you.

WILDEST THING

We will do some crazy things
To feel noticed or be seen.
The wildest thing I ever did
Was decide to just be me;

Disappearing to the crowds,
But noticed by a few,
And giving then the time I had
To those that saw me true.

THE IDEAL

Be thankful every day.
I swear I try to be,
But there are days I still fail
(If sharing honestly).

Still, I try and for this strive,
Seeking the ideal.
I give thanks even when
It's not what I first feel
And, from this daily practice, found
We will the ideal real.

Be thankful every day.
So I start mine now:
I'm thankful for this life,
For all I've come to know;
And—to everyone that's in it—
I pray my gratitude will show.

WHAT I'LL DO

I can't hang the stars.
I can't rope the moon,
But I can live my life
        so that
It is a light for you:

To shine on days when sadness shows,
Through times of hurt—that we all know;
To be the light you are to me;
To shine for you so that you see

How wonderful you are
When darkness blinds our sight;
To reassure in times of doubt
That all will be alright.

No, I can't hang the stars,
And I can't rope the moon;
But I can love you every day,
And that is what I'll do.

WHATEVER THAT BECOMES

Whatever that becomes,
I hope your day is bright;
That it holds and carries through
As light cedes into night;

That happiness, in you, resides
As you lay to rest,
Then resumes, in next day's dawn,
With life lived at its best:

Not as slogan, not as phrase
But simple acts, lived simple ways
That show one's joy and share one's heart.
Such is our choice, with every start

Of breaking light upon the Earth;
How do we choose to live?
What, of us, will we give
To spread Light cast by the Son
Throughout our days, at dawn begun?

I will choose to see known joys
Wherever they are found
And seek to spread them as I go
Like seeds upon the ground;

To take and root in other's lives;
To grow and bear new fruit:
Springing forth from simple seed
Of lived love's shining Truth.

#sharejoy

Whatever that becomes,
I hope your day is bright;
And that, in you, another sees
Your life's exudant light.

Byron McCoy

NEW LIGHT

On one of my darker days
I read a simple phrase:
"Be a light in this world"
That shone into my haze.

On her face, and in her smile,
Held goodness I could see;
And ever since that point of light
That's what I've tried to be.